Life... Create Your Own Masterpiece!

CHRISTINA THOEN

Balboa Press books may be ordered through booksellers or by contacting:

Balboa Press
A Division of Hay House
1663 Liberty Drive
Bloomington, IN 47403
www.balboapress.com
1 (877) 407-4847

ISBN: 978-1-4525-9944-1 (sc)
ISBN: 978-1-4525-9945-8 (e)

Library of Congress Control Number: 2015904496

Print information available on the last page.

Balboa Press rev. date: 08/19/2015

BALBOA.
PRESS
A DIVISION OF HAY HOUSE

Endorsements

"Wow Christina! I just finished reading your book … it was so amazing! I loved the flow, the energy … it was definitely a feel good read. I was blubbering like a baby when I read the Saint Christopher story. I can hardly wait to see it in print with all of your beautiful paintings complementing it. I will be the first in line to buy copies to give to all of my friends!"

—Mariana Sniezek, Registered nurse, Calgary, Alberta

"Good morning, Christina. I read your book last night and this morning, and it is absolutely amazing. You are a true inspiration as an artist and author. I can't wait to book a class that includes art and life lessons together."

—Bonnie Isaacson Marcoux, Life coach, Saskatoon, Saskatchewan

"With generous wisdom and positive energy, art principles such as balance, emphasis and proportion are illustrated with Christina's vibrant paintings and infectious enthusiasm in a refreshingly concise & accessible gem of a book."

—Elisabeth Soderberg, singer/songwriter, Toronto, Ontario

About the Cover Art

"Paris Spendor," acrylic painting, original size: 36 inches X 54 inches, 2010

This was painted soon after a trip to my favorite city in the world. I'm sure my love of Paris has to do with all the famous Impressionist artists who painted there in the past. The art culture is still so alive in Paris, and you can feel it in the air. The energy you feel taking a walk at night with all of the traffic and the people out on the street is exciting, and at the same time, it is warm and comforting. It's a totally feel-good place for me.

Dedication & Acknowledgments

Dedicated to our children—Anthony, Nathan, and Quinten—Thank you for being a huge and very special part of my life's masterpiece. You are the most amazing boys any parents could ever ask for and you teach us so much about life. You are so unique and perfectly yourselves. You make us so proud and we are super excited to see you create your own masterpieces! I wish you all the best in creating your own beautiful ones!

Special thanks to Mom and Dad. You gave me life and did your best in making me who I am today. Thank you for instilling and modeling empathy and giving. I am eternally grateful for your guidance, your love, and your unwavering belief in me.

To my sisters—Lis and Mariana—for being so much more than sisters. You are two of my best friends. I can share any secret with you and get advice from you. When we get together, we laugh so hard that our stomachs ache for days. I love that ache!

To all of the rest of my soul sisters—you know who you are! Thank you so much for being part of my life and for allowing me to be a part of yours. I love you all.

To my brother Kim for being with us for sixteen amazing years—and for teaching me so much about love and learning to live every day to its full. We know you're doing great where you are, but we all still really miss you and can't wait to see you again.

To my husband for being so wise, supportive, and loving. You tell me things I don't always want to hear. You are my true soul mate and my best friend, and I look forward to spending the rest of my life with you.

To God, I cannot thank you enough for your continual guidance and love.

*"Sun-Kissed," acrylic painting,
original size: 20" x 40", 2007*

"Sun-Kissed" was a spiritual painting for me. I was thinking of my children that day, and as I painted, a kiss appeared in the sky. Kisses are my signature as a parent. When our boys were little, I would always give them kisses and say, "Lipstick alert!" I would also kiss notes with lipstick before writing, "Love, Mom." This painting definitely reminds me of how we're being watched over from above and kissed every day!

Contents

Preface

About fifteen years ago, I noticed something when I was teaching art classes. In my art school, I constantly made analogies between how to create a great masterpiece in art as being the same in life. To help students understand, I would compare the learning in their artwork by giving them life scenarios they could relate to. It turns out that the important elements of art and principles of composition were really the same—whether we were talking about a beautiful painting or a life well lived.

I decided I needed to write this book, and I hoped it would help people find a new perspective on life and create the beautiful life of their dreams. I have yet to find someone not talented in art, and once they learn the basics and have some experience and practice, they are all able to create the most beautiful artwork. I knew this could also be true in everyone's lives. We are in control of the lives we create for ourselves, and we have the choice to make ours amazing! This book is a guide for doing just that!

"Home in Northern Saskatchewan," acrylic painting, original size: 36" x 54", 2013

This painting brings back fond memories of being north of Missinippi, canoeing with our family. The sunsets where we live in northern Saskatchewan are amazing. With all the lakes we have, it is a normal sight to see a beautiful sunset being reflected on water, which is what this painting is all about. Saskatchewan's slogan is "The Land of Living Skies," and I love seeing the beauty in our sky. When I think about our lives and dreams about our future, I often think, *"The sky's the limit!"* How exciting is that?

Introduction

So how does one create a masterpiece of their life? When you think of a great masterpiece, it means the artwork is aesthetically pleasing and has a depth that touches a part of your soul like great music does. To create a masterpiece of your life, the pleasing part is more about what happens inside of you (contentment, happiness, peace, etc.). *How many people long for happiness, but from the outside looking in, they seem to have everything? What creates happiness? What creates a song in your heart that you can't help but sing out to the world?*

Art? Why have I had this attraction? Why has this kept coming up in my life? I took it right back to the roots of what visual art has to do with. I finally figured it out. First of all, when you think of visual, what do you think of? Seeing? Yes, of course. And seeing happens to be one of the five senses. And what's important about your senses? They just happen to be THE most important part of being able to experience life! If you don't have your senses, you are definitely not living—or you are in a coma. That is HUGE…

> "To create a masterpiece of your life, the pleasing part is more about what happens inside of you (contentment, happiness, peace, etc.)."

When you really think about it, if you didn't experience life with your senses, you'd actually not be living a whole lot, would you? Therefore, when turning up any of the five senses, you actually have the opportunity to turn up your life a little bit. It is said that 80 percent of information we assimilate we assimilate through the senses is visual. (Khouw, 2006) This tells me that turning up the visual sense is important if you want to be able to experience more of your life. This is simple, and learning about art and being an artist does just that. Even musicians who mainly deal with the sense of sound, Joni Mitchell and Paul McCartney, have realized the power of the visual and do art as well. Joni Mitchell has regularly attested that she is a painter first and a musician second.

You could choose to be an art collector. This turns up your sense of seeing to a degree because you are stimulating the sense of seeing as you choose and discriminate between different styles of art with your choices. The presence of color is important in interior environments since most people spend more time inside than outside. Many people don't realize why art is such an important part of your life, and if you've ever been in a room with bare walls, you know this is true.

Being an art collector is great, and creating a positive space definitely improves the interior environment in your home. However, learning how to be an artist especially enhances this sense of seeing, and if you have the inkling, it will expand your life even more.

Unfortunately, many people either don't think they have the ability—or they don't choose to try to refine their skills. The amazing thing is that most people do have the ability and just need some coaching. I feel that everyone is an artist, but they just have different styles. After teaching art to hundreds of students, I have yet to find someone who isn't talented in art.

At ten years old, I knew I wanted to be an artist. I've always said children are so wise. I'm so thankful that I was given the gift of an experience one day on our farm that helped me stay true to my dream. I found a beautiful painting in the shed, and when I asked my mom who painted it, she said it was her. I was so perplexed because I'd never seen her paint. I asked her why she quit painting, and she said she just got busy, got married, had children, and didn't have the time to paint.

I vowed at that moment that no matter what happened in my future, I would always take time to create art. And more than thirty-five years later, I can say that I've kept that promise to myself. A beautiful side note is that since my parents moved to Prince Albert seven years ago, my mom started taking art classes with me after not painting for more than fifty years!

Life's a place to experience and grow, to learn and become new, to have fun, and enjoy the adventure. Everyone has the ability to thrive. Just like trees, we never really quit growing during our lifetimes. If there's a dry year, the tree may not grow as much, but luckily people aren't trees. We always have a choice. I can't imagine a life without art. When you think back to the cave paintings, people have been creating art since the beginning of time.

Teaching art is similar to teaching about life. Some people are perceptive to growth and learning and are like sponges. Others who have some innate talent and seemingly master it easily, but they are quick to quit when they think they have the essentials. These are the same people who generally can't cope and tend to crash and burn when there is true learning to do or challenges ahead. They may stay in the same comfortable spot without moving forward and not create true happiness. A goal I've always had in life is to learn one new thing a day. I can't say I've always reached it, but it is something I strive for.

> "Life's a place to experience and grow—to learn and become new, to have fun and enjoy the adventure. Everyone has the ability to be thriving."

I love art, and I love everything about it. I love creating art, and I love teaching art. I will never forget the man who came into my studio one day, looked at the tables, and asked what I did there. I explained that I taught art classes.

He pointed to one of my paintings and said, "You should be painting—not teaching art."

I felt as if someone had stabbed me. *How could I not share this lovely thing with others?* To me, it feels like a gift. *Why would I not want to give this gift to others?* As an art teacher, I love to see people grow, change, become more rounded, develop more understanding, and become more accepting of others and their differences. More importantly, I love to see them embrace themselves and their unique art styles. Just like anything, it requires work and continued learning. As always, the work you put into things makes them worthwhile.

I always wondered why I loved creating art. No one in my family did artwork. After my first trip to Paris, I told my sister about how it felt like home—even though I don't even speak French. I thought it was so strange. She said I must have been a master painter in a past life. I'll never know, but I definitely feel a strong connection to the Impressionists, especially Vincent Van Gogh.

It wasn't until I was getting my blood taken in a downstairs clinic in Prince Albert that I finally figured out why art is so important in our lives. Even before I was getting the life taken out of me (*yes, my blood!*), I noticed that I felt depleted and half dead. The waiting room was so drab; with so many bare walls, the room had no life at all. I actually felt bad for the nurses who had to work in that environment day after day. I knew how it must make them feel. That was when I figured out what art on your walls does for you. It livens up your room and livens you up too! The explanation of exactly why comes later in this book.

I have wanted to write this book since I first started teaching art lessons and realized how similar learning to be a great artist is like learning how to live a great life. I believe it must be somehow related to being created and being given a life by the Creator (God). We often talk of artists being creators. This book has been in my mind for fifteen years and I started writing it ten years ago. I wasn't in a hurry to finish because I wanted to be wise enough to create a book that could help people. I'm sure hoping it does!

Right down to the perspective and the way you look at things, learning to be a great artist is all about learning to see. By reading this book, you will understand how living a great life is all about that too. We tend to take things for granted and walk through the forest without seeing the trees for most of our lives. It is hard to believe that when we pay attention to the details—and the small things in life—we start to learn to live a much fuller life with much more happiness and contentment.

Just think for a moment about a toddler taking a walk. They take their time and stop and look at everything. They also always have huge smiles on their faces! We need to keep our learning fresh and keep paying attention. We need to keep interested and stay in awe of the world around us!

"Right down to the perspective and the way you look at things, learning to be a great artist is all about learning to see. By reading this book, you will understand how living a great life is all about that too."

Another really important thing that every artist needs to learn is that you can never compare your work to anyone else's. Each person has a unique style that they must accept, embrace, and let grow. This is true with life too. Each one of us has an opportunity to do something great in this world and with our lives, which no one else can do. We each have unique personalities, upbringings, and a combination of the age-old mixture of environment and heredity that make us who we are today. It's simple. An apple tree can't grow the same as an orange tree, doesn't look like an orange tree, and won't produce the same fruit either! We need to embrace the "tree" that we are—unique and original!

I have taught hundreds of students, and I have yet to find anyone who has no talent for art. This tells me that we also all have the talent to create great lives if we choose to learn and put in the effort to do so. The biggest things are a willingness to learn and the motivation and understanding that inspires a continued learning process.

We need to have a lifelong journey where new knowledge never ends. We have witnessed few master artists, such as Michelangelo, or famous people who experienced a great life, such as Mother Teresa, when you count up the number of people who have lived on this world since its creation. There should and could be a whole lot more. These amazing people knew they would never learn all they wanted or needed to in one lifetime. Throughout their lives, they challenged themselves to continue growing and learning. Michelangelo, on his deathbed at eighty-nine, said he was just starting to learn the alphabet of his profession. Now there's someone who really knew about learning! Again, it's all about choice.

"We need to have a life long journey where
new knowledge never ends."

"The Road Home," acrylic painting, original size: 21" x 27", 2006

This painting makes me think that anything is possible. The clouds are all white and fluffy, and it looks like the perfect day for an adventure. We know it's going to be fun because our sights are set on the sky, which is full of dreams, and the horizon, which tells us we can go pretty much anywhere we want! We need to start out the day with a twinkle in our eyes, thoughts of gratitude for the day—the gift that it is—and excitement about what we can experience and learn! Let's get started! No matter where we go, we can choose the roads we travel and the roads we choose to go home!

Preparation—Getting Your Materials and Supplies Ready to Begin!

Good Attitude—Positive

So, how do you begin? First of all, you need to put on your rose-colored glasses. I've had more than one friend tell me that I wear them. At first, I took it as an insult. It sounded as though I was naive. It wasn't until later that I realized that it is actually a gift. It really means looking at things positively—without negativity—which is a choice you make. It goes back to your perspective on how you see things.

You can decide what to pay attention to and what to ignore, according to your choices. I tend to focus on the light and not the dark. You have a choice with what type of attitude you carry with you daily. As artists, we often talk about the fear of the blank canvas. It's that feeling we get when we are first starting a painting. I'm not sure that feeling ever goes away—no matter how long you've been painting.

Fear is always going to be the biggest obstacle to creating what you want to create. Fear has been hardwired into our brains since cavemen were trying to survive, but we must get past it. There are many ways to do that, but the most powerful way is through love and appreciation. Just being grateful for everything in your life makes your fears take a hike! It takes courage to rise above fear.

Just like the Nike advertisement, you need to "Just do it!" I often ask myself, *"What is the worst thing is that could happen?"* Once I think about all the scenarios and consequences, "doing it" is always the right answer.

"Rose Colored Glasses," acrylic painting, original size: 14" x 18", 2004

This painting was painted in Bali when we were traveling with our children. It is a self-portrait that reminds me of the importance of seeing the world from a positive perspective because you have that choice in every moment of every day! Everyone can put on a pair of these glasses if they choose, and the more people who wear them, the happier our world will be!

Healthy Balance—Mind/Body/Spirit

Second, to create a great life, you need to be in a healthy state of mind. This happens from the day-to-day choices you make to look after yourself. First, you need to eat right, take your vitamins, and exercise daily to nurture your body. Have some fun—and don't forget a bit of yoga, meditation, and prayer. In a nutshell, work hard, play hard, and remember to rest and relax a little in between. It's amazing how many people don't get enough sleep. Changing this one simple thing will make a world of difference in their life.

When the exercise in art class is taking time to see the details in our subject, I call it "insightful meditation." We look for the tiny details in things while our minds meditate on the subject. Even as little as five minutes of meditation can connect you to that place inside that is full of wisdom and insights. It can help with day-to-day choices and challenges because when your mind is quiet, questions are often answered.

People love retreats and going to a cabin at the lake to let go and de-stress, but you can learn to take this trip in your mind. Going for a walk is another great way to clear our minds, relax, and open up to our inner wisdom. If you can take the time to write in a journal, you will also find many insights into your life. For many people, writing things down gives them a clearer picture of what's really going on. A great exercise is to write down the things you'd like to see in your life. It's amazing how those things will tend to show up once you've had the intention and have written them down. This has worked for me many times!

Keep humor in your life. Make sure you always have some fun; otherwise, things can become too serious and feel stagnant. Try to have some good belly laughs every day. Humor shifts your perspective and lifts your heart; it is great medicine on any day. You can test this by seeing if you can laugh and be sad (feeling your heavy heart) at the same time. It's impossible!

Getting together with good friends for some soul food always feels amazing, and another great way of lifting your spirits is spending time with children. One of my favorite things to do is hang out with my great nieces and nephews. The love in their hearts, sparkles in their eyes, and unending fascination and excitement for life are contagious! Don't forget to plan holidays, and like a teenager, continue to be excited for the weekend because of something fun you will enjoy! Health and happiness depend on each other, and we need to focus on both. Most importantly, remember to always take care for yourself first. You can't fill anyone else's cup if yours isn't full. Take some time for just you—you won't regret it!

Make sure you take a little time for listening to music and dancing every now and then in your life. It's interesting that music also feeds your soul. It can take you to different times and places. We all know how great music can make us feel and how great it feels to dance. Go for it! This is sure to put a spring in your every step!

Your home needs to be your sanctuary. It's important to create a great environment by paying attention to wall colors and hanging some great artwork on your walls to touch your soul. Your favorites that make you feel happy should be hung where you spend most of your time.

"A Beautiful World,"
acrylic painting,
original size: 24"
x 36", 2006

This painting signifies to me the relationship between mind, body, and soul and the beauty created when all are in harmony within their environment. This is when all great things happen, and it reminds me of the delicate balance for a life well lived. The mind is the flowers reaching for the light, the fruit is the soul carrying the seeds of forever, and the vase is the body in its fragility. This painting makes me realize that you can only pop out the window and explore the world in all of its beauty when these are in harmony!

Plan—Working toward a Lifetime Plan

Third, you need to figure out your plan. This means figuring out what you were put on this earth to do. For some, this can take a lot of contemplation and a lot of time. For others, it's more like happy accidents, which also happens while doing artwork. The person doesn't seem to have to work too hard or take much time to figure it out, and it just seems to be there. This most often happens because they've always followed their hearts.

Years ago, a friend of mine in a business class gave me *Do What You Love, The Money Will Follow* by Marsha Sinetar. The reality of the book's message was definitely true for me. I think I have been blessed because my life did call me in directions. I didn't spend a lot of time trying to figure it out because I've always followed my heart without question. The only problem is that I can still sometimes have self-doubt in my head. I wonder if I'm on the right track—even though my heart really does know it's right. I think that is just human nature. We tend to question ourselves, and it's about getting used to knowing the difference between a true question and a needless fear-based one! There isn't any person on this earth who doesn't experience those moments. Again, we need to conquer the old fear part of our brain when it kicks in.

If you just can't figure it out, think back to when you were young. It's helpful to put your hand on your heart while you ask these questions. *What made you most happy? What did you enjoy doing? Who were you with? Were you by yourself? Where were you? Were you inside or outside? What do you find really easy that others find hard?* Think about the one thing that you do where time slips away—that is your passion! *Why did you enjoy doing it so much?* After answering those questions, you'll be able to start to figure it out. At ten years old, you totally knew what made your heart sing. Often we forget that with time.

Sometimes you need someone else to figure it out for you (sort of like an art critic) because you are so close to yourself. It can be really hard to be objective. Also we're our own worst critics so often that we don't believe we have what it takes when we really do. We can really be hard on ourselves and not have the belief in ourselves to do what we are really called for, but the truth is you really do know inside what is right for you. If something feels bad, it is bad, and if it feels right, it is right. This may take some practice to relearn since we all had these instincts as children. Learn to trust that gut feeling that is almost always right. Doing what you do because of listening to internal messages is more important than listening to external messages. So many of us do this, basing ourselves and our actions on what others say, and what they think of us.

Between the ages of eight and twelve, we are most "ourselves" before much influence from others has taken place. Research has shown that between the ages of eight and twelve, it is important to start learning about art and continue with instruction; otherwise, fear starts to set in. Without help, many will quit doing art. The truth is, people of any age have the power to make choices and the freedom to make those choices. We can take responsibility and take action at any time. We can create our own destinies and plan for them, but we can't be passive in doing that. The older we are, the more we need to push past the fear because it tends to grow with age.

Sometimes it might feel like your life plan and your dreams can never come true. *Never say never.* Send your requests and dreams into the world. It is amazing what will happen when you have a positive mindset and believe. You bring about the things you think about. Keep your thoughts on your desires—not on what you don't want happening.

Since our three boys were little, my husband and I talked about how awesome it would be to take a year off of work and take our boys traveling. It turned out that we did just that! *Were we any different than anyone else as far as how much money we were making to be able to do it?* No. We just had a dream and decided to take the risk and go for it. Our kids were ten, thirteen, and fifteen and that time with them was so precious. We will never regret that decision even though it meant we had to remortgage the house in order to go. Once we made the decision, it was like dominoes. Everything fell into place in order for it to happen. It was definitely one of the best decisions we ever made.

Know that you truly can expect your dreams to come true. That doesn't mean there isn't some hard work and planning involved. It just means that if you want something badly enough, you pretty much can make it happen—even if it seems to start off slowly. Focus on what you want and all of the "hows" will figure themselves out!

> "Never say never. Send your requests and dreams into the world. It is amazing what will happen when you have a positive mindset and believe."

So what if you don't really have a plan, but you kind of have an idea? It's best to get started. Your plan will often evolve if you are heading in the right direction. The blank page in art is always the scariest, but just like anything, once you get started, it's not so scary. The challenge can be fun. Think of it as freedom—the freedom to create whatever you want!

If you continue to follow your heart, everything will work out. Focus on how you want to feel—and imagine yourself feeling that way. All the details won't be there yet, and that is why you won't feel like you really know what you're doing. It will get more refined as you go. All you need to do is trust yourself. Fear is the one thing that you must erase from your thoughts. It's also what cripples many artists. Focus on your strengths and ignore your weaknesses. No one has ever built a great life or created great artwork by focusing on or trying to fix personal weaknesses. *Forget them!* We all have them, but your strengths are where your future dreams are. DREAM BIG! You are the most powerful dream life creator!

The harder the climb, the higher you go—and the more you will learn. It will be all worth it at the end. I've always told our children to shoot for the stars and know that the world is their oyster. There will be times when artists want to throw out their artwork, and there will be times you will want to give up on things that are hard in your life. Once you get to the top, it will be so worth your efforts.

You need to be optimistic and know that everything happens for a reason. Even during the moments where you feel the pain of falling down, realize that the greater the pain, the greater the lesson. This gives you a feeling of power over past regrets and future fears. Never lose sight of the big picture—even during the tough times. We all experience them. Lessons are for learning, and they need to be part of the journey. Embrace the lessons. Know they are part of your amazing dream life!

> "Never lose sight of the big picture—even during the tough times. We all experience them. Lessons are for learning, and they need to be part of the journey."

I compare life to being a swimmer in an ocean. Sometimes some pretty big waves come and you feel like giving up, but this is when it's most important to hang on and do what you need to do. Before you know it, it all calms down and you have had a great learning experience. Remember, the bigger the wave, the more learning you've experienced. Once you have survived a huge wave in your life, you will have a lot more confidence to know that you can handle any wave that comes your way. In some ways, you are fortunate because the smaller waves will feel like nothing! Be thankful for the big waves. You might think you're drowning, but in reality, you will feel much more freedom in knowing your strengths and what you are capable of. You could also compare it to climbing a mountain. The bigger the mountain, the more struggle, but check out the view from the top!

"Sunrise at Emma Lake," acrylic painting, original size: 24" x 36", 2013

This painting signifies the journey ahead and the freedom to choose which direction to go in life. This world we live in is rich with opportunities. It also reminds me that when you get out on the water, there will always be winds that come up and waves to go through. This is also the fun part, depending on how you look at it and whether you enjoy rapids! Once you get through them, you will be exhilarated from the excitement of learning your own power and strengths. You will begin to look forward to the next adventure, knowing you can totally handle whatever comes your way!

Preparation Exercises

First, you need to KNOW that you can do this! FORGET all your limiting thoughts in your mind before you begin! During art classes, we talk about this. We also talk a lot about how you will be your own worst critic. If you've never had real art classes, there's no reason to have any thought about whether or not you can be a great artist.

Most things in life come down to your beliefs. The beautiful thing is that you can change those beliefs! My job as an art teacher is to build confidence and help students believe they can do it! After the hump, it's all downhill. The fear steps aside, and the desire to learn and grow becomes the focus! In your life, I suggest you write down a list of all the negative things you can think of in your past that you didn't like and don't want to be part of your future. Then burn the paper… It's a way to symbolize your "new" life, which isn't held down by any old beliefs or moments in your life that drag you down.

> "Most things in life come down to your beliefs. The beautiful thing is that you can change those beliefs!"

In art, we will often do a few sketches (also called studies) to get the feel of what we're going to create. This just gets you started, and once you've started, the rest becomes easy. In your life, this is true too. If you have a goal in mind, just start taking steps toward it. When you start, things "happen"… Every time I start a new painting, I know it's going to get done. The starting is often the hardest part because I know the work involved and know I'm committed to finishing.

Another great exercise for creating the future you want is by visualizing and feeling it. The greatest power your mind has is using your imagination. You can create something you want in your future by picturing it in your mind. Don't forget to feel *(a great big smile on your face helps!)*. I've always believed that *WHAT YOU FEEL BECOMES REAL!*

Some people like to make vision boards. They cut out pictures or words that represent how they want their lives to look in the future. Another thing I suggest, which is a little more concrete, is a future chest, where you put articles or symbols of things you'd like to see in your future! Take a few minutes a day to *imagine* your perfect life in the future! *What does your perfect life look like? Where are you and what are you doing? How does that big smile on your face feel?*... Those few minutes will come back to you tenfold—and you are so worth the time!

"Where Canada Began," acrylic painting, original size: 36" x 48", 2012

This painting is of the Canada Building in Charlottetown. That is where the papers were signed by all of the provinces to create Canada! Imagine the dreams and aspirations of these men as they thought about their new country and what it would mean for the people living there in the future. They had a vision. Lucky us!

Elements of Art

The elements of art are essentially the basic building blocks of all art. These are the parts in artwork that make up the whole piece. The elements include the line, shape, value, color, texture, and space.

When choosing your subject, the most important thing is that you LOVE it. You need to love it so much that when you are really tired of it and are getting tired of the learning—*and it's taking more time than you thought*—that you'll have the patience to hang on and keep working on it! I've noticed that most young children choose pets, such as dogs and cats, for subjects. This shouldn't be a surprise since children are full of wisdom and intuitively want to love and be loved… They know that pets give unwavering love and loyalty and are excellent additions to a life well lived.

Many artists focus on nature as their subjects. Being out in nature renews our spirits. Instinctually, people love having artwork depicting nature on their walls because they know it can take them to a different place and give them what they need when they can't really be there *(almost like a mini-vacation for the soul)*. My favorite subjects are landscapes (mostly trees and skies) and street scenes. I love the tranquil energy of nature, and I also love the high energy of a city. They are opposites, but I love the contrast and experience of both! It's interesting that traveling to new cities and new places in nature have always been important parts of my life journey. Of course, it makes sense that these are also my favorite subjects in art!

When students who have just started learning art have a relative or friend ask them to do a specific painting or drawing, it tends to completely stifle their excitement for the piece and becomes a struggle for them. It's taken me years to enjoy doing commissioned pieces, but I'm also picky about to what pieces I agree to do because I know I need to love them. It's no different in life… People need to make their own choices about what they want to do in their lives—*no matter how their family and friends feel about it*. You can't live your life for others, and you can't go about your life trying to meet someone else's expectations instead of your own. Life is all about YOU—and you need to never forget that.

"Urban Wonder," acrylic painting, original size 48" x 72", 2013

This painting of downtown Ottawa at night brings back great memories of a family vacation. We had such a great time experiencing all Ottawa has to offer. When we were there, I felt patriotic and happy to live in Canada. Once we were home, I couldn't wait to get started on this piece! It was my way of re-experiencing a great memory! Going on holidays to new places brings me a lot of happiness and has always been a part of my life's planning and goals. The planning and anticipation is as a much a part of the excitement as the trip itself—*the journey and the memories are just as important as the destination!*

Step 1: Line and Shape—Drawing Out Your Subject

If you're following your heart, the lines and shapes you put down will be ones that won't really change a lot in the end. You need to take your time with this. These are things that are in line with your morals and values, and they don't really change over time. This means defining important things and separating them (business, personal, work, etc.). This includes choosing a life partner, a career, and the place you live and put down roots.

You choose "what and who is important in your life." These must be things you truly love because they hold true throughout life, and you'll need the patience to continue to deal with them. It will be important for you to have enjoyment as you go. Here is where you must "pick a scene" you will never tire of. Choose one you feel a *strong* connection to. In artwork, this is your subject. You'll need to balance the horizontal lines (the peaceful, easygoing ones) with the vertical (upright and responsible) ones. You'll need to balance a variety of shapes, including the round, loving ones and the ones with sharp corners that push you to change and grow.

In art, you need to draw the largest shapes first; otherwise, your proportions can be off and you might not have room for all of your shapes. The same is true in life… You need to have an idea about what you want in your life. Make sure you concentrate on the really big things first; otherwise, it's easy to get distracted by all the little things. You can run out of time for the big things that really matter! It seems to me that our technology now can easily burn up time, and we need to be careful about how we use it—and how much we use it! There's a finite amount of time in your life, and there is a finite amount of room on your canvas for your lines and shapes. Be selective!

> "You need to have an idea about what you want in your life. Make sure you concentrate on the really big things first; otherwise, it's easy to get distracted by all the little things. You can run out of time for the big things that really matter!"

It is always possible to change your lines and shapes down the road. However, if you have ever done a home renovation, you know that taking out walls requires work on the ceilings and floors. Changing later on is always a *lot* of work. So take your time setting up your lines and shapes. You want to have the love there so you have the patience to work through any difficulties that arise in the future!

The initial lines and shapes are the building blocks of your life. Once you begin your life journey, it is often harder to change some of those initial choices. For example, it is never too late to go back to school, but it is definitely harder to go back later in life. If you choose to take your education early in life when the timing is right, it makes life a lot smoother than if you decide later that you'd like to go back to school. With a family, this choice later in life is probably more challenging, but if it is part of your plan, it is *never ever* too late!

When teaching about drawing a line, I often talk about having to know where point A (your starting point), and point B (your ending point) are. This tells you where you are beginning and where you'll end. It is like finding your goals. You need to know where you want to end up. Otherwise, you'll be traveling along without really knowing where you're going.

Beginning with the end in mind really helps put you on the right road. If you think about it as planning a trip, you absolutely need to know where your destination is and whether you want to go through certain cities along the way. You need to decide what you want as part of your life's journey. Once you decide your destination or goal, you can begin your journey and decide what you want to see along the way.

In art, the most amazing part is when people are finished their artwork—it often looks way better than the reference image they were working from. In life, the same is true… When you put out an intention for what you'd like to have happen, when your dreams come true, they are often even better than what you expected!

"Holy Times," original painting, original size: 24" x 24", 2014

This painting was commissioned and speaks about putting in the things in life that nourish us and feed our souls. It's so easy to get distracted in life, but taking this important time of quiet renewal for ourselves—*either alone or with the people we most care about*—gives us a chance to set the course of our lives and what we feel is important. Downtime is just as important so we can do some deep thinking and take the time to plan and dream our futures!

Step 2: Value and Color—Working on the Basic Colors and Light Source

Once you have your basic lines and shapes down, you need to focus on your value *(the way light hits your subject)*. When teaching art, I say that this is the most important part of artwork. I also believe it is the most important part of life. To me, this really means your spirituality or the way light hits your life! In artwork, the *light* brings *life* to the piece. Without it, everything seems gloomy, flat, and lifeless. The same is true with life—it becomes enlightened when light is shed on things, and there is much greater understanding.

In scientific terms, light is energy, and it is absolutely necessary for life and crucial for plants to live and grow. Therefore, it is essential for all life on this planet to flourish. It is similar to having "light" in your life. You will truly feel this energy inside yourself when you nurture your spirituality. You won't feel like you're *in the dark*, and you'll feel bright and much more happy and content. When you are full of light, this light is reflected onto others, and they too will feel its glow.

In scientific terms, light is energy, and it is absolutely necessary for life and crucial for plants to live and grow. Therefore, it is essential for all life on this planet to flourish. It is similar to having "light" in your life. You will truly feel this energy inside yourself when you nurture your spirituality.

For myself personally it means keeping faith as part of my daily life. This can be a touchy subject for some, and most have to experience for themselves what this means. An amazing "life fullness" unfolds when people have faith. As much as you want to share your light, you have to be careful not to *shine the lightbulb* in others' eyes. No one likes that, and for some people, it is uncomfortable and will in fact rather turn them away. Even Pope Francis recently spoke of the importance of not proselytizing, but rather wanted the church to grow by attraction.

No one likes being told how to think or what to do. Often just being a living example can be the best gift you can give others. It makes others curious about your glow. When they ask you why you are so happy *(which they will!)*, you can start a conversation about your faith. This may be a radical thought, but I've always felt there is only one God… So maybe the car I travel in is a Christian, and the car my friend in Bali travels in is a Hindu. I've always felt we were going to the same place and that I'll meet her in "heaven."

For most people, it's due to where they are born and what family raised them, but at a certain age, faith also becomes a personal choice. For me, a car makes travel a lot easier—and it's much nicer than walking alone. However, a lot of people experience their own personal faith without any organized religion. Some prefer to refer to God as the Supreme Being, Divine Intelligence, Spirit, or the Universe. To each his own… You need to choose what's right for you. Some are still searching for what works for them, and they will know when they find it because peace and contentment will set in. It won't be a brief good feeling that happens after a material purchase or a fun event. It will be a daily continual *flow* and *glow* that just feels good! No one's chosen faith is ever right or wrong. They will know when it's right for them.

In artwork, showing the light is absolutely crucial. It makes your artwork three-dimensional and creates depth. It makes a simple circle become a sphere… It makes your work look lifelike and real enough to pretend walk into! Having faith makes your life whole and gives it depth. Until you experience it, you may not completely understand what all the fuss is about…

It's difficult to talk about value without talking about color. When you shine light through a prism, you get the rainbow of colors. So in fact, color is light! Because light is energy, we know that color is energy too! Hanging a painting with pure pigment is like adding a window into your home—without a renovation! The painting carries *light energy*.

Values of colors really mean hues of colors. Each color changes from light shades to darker shades depending on how much light is in it. When colors are held closest to you, they are brightest. Color energy has been used as therapy for years. A person is treated with color in order to balance some type of physical or mental imbalance. Chakras are an example of how we are full of color and full of energy. When you are not in balance, disease and things like that become part of your life. When we are balanced and healthy, we have the full spectrum and the characteristics of each color in our lives.

I know that when I put on my pink polka-dotted T-shirt, I automatically feel happier. That is because pink is the color of love. If I wear red a lot—since it's the highest-energy color—I feel a little extra energy within myself. I might even find myself getting agitated. There's a reason why bulls run toward the matador in the red cape! Green is a great color for healing and caring. Orange is a social and fun color. Yellow is a color of intelligence. Purple is for creativity and inspiration. The warm colors automatically make you feel cozier, and the cooler colors make you feel more airy and carefree. Choosing the colors in your home, clothing, and spaces around you influences how you feel from day to day. In artwork, you must be aware of color influences as well. Too much red in a painting is too *in your face* and takes over the rest of the work. It is similar to cayenne pepper in cooking or choosing to skydive every day! It takes over and you can lose the appreciation and "flavor" of other "quiet" yet important things.

> "Color is light! Because light is energy, we know that color is energy too! Hanging a painting with pure pigment is like adding a window into your home—without a renovation! The painting carries "light energy."

People often ask me, "What about prints?" and I always ask this question, *"Do you prefer live bands or listening to CDs?"* The difference is similar. A painting made with pure pigment carries true energy in it versus synthetic chemically made colors for printing. Hanging a print on your wall will never create the feeling of warmth that an original will. You can actually feel the difference when standing in front of an original painting versus a print. Part of what you feel is also the energy the artist put into the creating piece. The bonus is the subject itself, which also carries an energy representing what the piece is about.

Once, at an art gallery in Las Vegas, I came around the corner and when I saw a painting, I immediately teared up and started crying before I even saw the artist's name. I found out that Van Gogh painted it when he was in an insane asylum during the last days of his life. His sadness came through as part of the energy in the painting. It's a good idea to do a little research when buying artwork so you know the kind of energy you are bringing into your home.

I'll never forget when a client stopped me on the street to tell me she had bought a piece of my art at a recent show. She told me that every time she looks at it, it makes her happy. I'm fortunate to have a positive, optimistic outlook on life, and I am so happy my paintings carry that energy. I have learned that I can only paint when I'm feeling great. Once I tried to paint when I wasn't feeling good emotionally, and in the end, I couldn't even look at the painting. I ended up destroying it.

"I'm fortunate to have a positive, optimistic outlook on life, and I am so happy my paintings carry that energy. I have learned that I can only paint when I'm feeling great."

When creating art, we have three choices for color patterns: monochromatic, harmonizing, or complementary. In any relationship with another person, the same is true. We choose relationships with people all of the time, and it's best to have a balance of close friends and family to help us grow and develop into the people we know we can be.

Monochromatic means one color is used with all the shades and highlights of white, gray, and black. This is a serene and comfortable type of art that is often used for spas and Zen areas. This color pattern has the least amount of energy. Therefore, in a relationship, the least amount of growth will happen with each other, but being together will be comfortable, which makes us feel content.

Harmonizing color patterns are when the colors from a portion of the color wheel are used. This means that there is a little bit of energy pull from these close colors; however there is generally a lot of harmony and similarity. There is a little more energy created.

Complementary color patterns are the most widely used for artists—and for the relationships many people find themselves in. Complementary colors are opposites on the wheel, but when they are side by side, they create energy in each other. It is like there is an unseen friction when they are put next to each other, which makes the colors stand out. These relationships create a lot of challenging moments, but they also offer the biggest opportunities for huge growth and change.

In art class, I say, *"Nothing is without consequence to everything else around it."* The most amazing thing I've learned about color is that two things next to each other will affect the other's color. For example, an apple will reflect red on a yellow banana, making an orangey color. This is also true in life! Who you spend the most time with definitely affects you and your life. Making the right choices about the people close to you is huge! People who never expect good things will often complain, and they never let go of their negative lessons. More negativity follows because that is what they choose to focus on. These are people to keep at a distance. You don't need their negative energy!

"Glowing Spirit," acrylic painting, original size: 18" x 24", 2005

This painting was my attempt at showing someone glowing. It's about the reality that we are all full of light—not darkness—but we have to choose to see that. We are spiritual and connect to a divine being (God). We feel the most full of light when we make efforts to keep these connections and develop deeper relationships. We know how we feel inside when we feel most alive and full of color—we want to share it like children do! Here's to love! Let us sparkle with shimmering light. Let us shine!

Step 3: Texture and Space—Detailed Foreground & Fuzzy Background

Once you have your lines, shapes, values, and colors in place, you can start to add texture and space. Texture refers to how things feel. You need to pay attention to the things that feel good and those that don't. Leonardo da Vinci always used to wear velour clothing because it felt so good. He was aware of how things around him felt and how they affected his feelings.

When things are close, you can really see their texture. As an artist, defining this texture is the most laborious and time-consuming part of the overall artwork. The truth is, this is also probably the easiest part of the artwork. Fitting in the pieces of what you see takes time, but it doesn't take the same amount of skill as drawing lines and shapes. You've done your texture work well when a viewer wants to touch your artwork. Tactile quality is appealing and attractive. As an artist, you are a magician… in fact, an illusionist! Focus on the highly textured parts of your work—and in your life. These choices require a lot of time and attention to make them highlights in your life. A framing customer of mine said, "*If you take care of the details, everything else will take care of itself.*"

Texture is only noticed close up. The closer you are to the texture, the more you are able to imagine how something feels by looking at it. We can tell how something will feel by how the light hits it. Again, it seems everything goes back to how light affects it. With something really furry or soft, the light drops in between the fibers. You don't really get a chance to see the light reflect much. If the surface is hard and shiny, you will be able to see the light reflecting a lot. Chrome and other metals really shine.

When we touch something, we get a chance to understand exactly how it feels. The cool thing is that you don't have to physically touch things in order to know how they feel because we already have background knowledge about how light works without even having to know it in a real conscious sense. This is the same with faith and other amazing things like love… You can't put your finger on them; you can only know them to be true by what they reflect back to you and how they affect you.

Space refers to how far and close things are from you. Choose things and people that are "important" to you and that feel good to be around close to you. Leave others at a distance. Some people seem happiest being unhappy. Those people are difficult to be around when you want to be happy. Pay extra attention to the people and things that *are* close to you because these matter the most. Don't focus on people and things that don't really matter to you. It's an absolute waste of time. The "things" that surround you in your home should also be ones that you love and cherish—get rid of anything that has any negative vibe attached to it.

Making choices may include decisions about family and friends that you love. You can choose to spend less time around them if you know they "bring you down." As you get close to people, you see more details, including their mistakes, flaws, and shortcomings (which we all have). It is important that you really love these people and that they jive with your morals and values, (lines, and shapes). That way, you will be able to accept their faults.

All colors, shapes, and details are brighter and more distinct up close. The saying *"The grass is greener on the other side of the fence,"* is absolutely not true. According to physics, colors are always brightest when they are closest to you. I often refer to close-up texture as showing the details because these details give you an idea about how something might feel. If the details you spend so much time on are the things that really matter, then you are doing a fine job. Your time and energy should be put into the things and people that are closest to you. Consider what those details might be. *Is it cleaning your house? Is it taking the time to do something special for those you love? Is it choosing to do a kind deed? Is it scrubbing out your cupboard? Is it having your hair done? Is it doing nice things without anyone else really needing to know about it? What do you focus in on?*

With distance, everything disappears, including lines, shapes, color, value, and textures. You can always choose what you want to focus on and what you push into the distance (what you choose not to have as part of your life). It is always *your choice…*

David Leffel said, *"Paying attention is the secret to life, and it's the secret to painting too."* Focus on what matters… Have you ever noticed that you have diamonds on the back of your hand? If you look closely, you will see those lines and shapes. Life has so many hidden diamonds. We just need to pay more attention. Taking the time to notice the details in your life that are special helps you gain perspective on your life. If you go about your day recognizing the beauty around you and paying less attention to the things that cause you heartache or are problems, you will feel a special shift inside, which can only be positive! Your focus will create your feelings so be sure to only go for the "good" stuff!

"Life has so many hidden diamonds. We just need to pay more attention. Taking the time to notice the details in your life that are special helps you gain perspective on your life."

"City Lights," acrylic painting, original size: 36" x 54", 2013

This painting is of downtown Prince Albert. The interesting thing is that everyone who looked at it, including the people who purchased it, thought it was in Paris because a lot of my street scenes are of Paris. It's interesting to see that the most special sights can be in your own backyard. You just need to be on the lookout for them—even on wet, rainy nights!

Principles of Composition

What is composition? Composition is how an artist organizes his or her elements—the lines, shapes, colors, values, textures, and spaces. They organize it in such a way that it is most "aesthetically pleasing". Photographers often use the *rule of thirds* to compose. Masters in art have used the *golden ratio* or *phi,* which has historically been thought of as divine since its principles show up in nature all of the time.

In your life, this means how you organize your life—what you want it to look like, what you want to be part of your life, what to prioritize, what things are important, what things in your life are more in the background, etc. When we think about composing in music, it is about creating the notes that sound beautiful together. Let's see what the principles of composition are and how they relate to your life.

"Sydney Opera House," acrylic painting, original size: 24" x 36", 2007

This painting brings back great memories of a time with our boys when we were traveling and exploring. The Sydney Opera House in Australia was built on the principles of phi, and that magical calculation is felt when you are close to the building. When I look at this painting, it reminds me of three jewels in my life: our family, traveling and music!

Emphasis

Emphasis is the first principle of composition. When you think about it, we absolutely need to decide what to emphasize in our lives. Choose what's important to highlight, and spend your time on it. *What will you choose to do as a career? It will have a huge emphasis in your life and leaving a legacy is always a feel good thing to do, but will it be your primary focus?*

The emphasis in artwork is always what your eyes focus in on first within the piece. *Where do your eyes go first when* you *look at a painting? What is the focal point that takes your attention right away?* We are drawn to faces, especially the eyes because they tell the stories of our souls. By looking at someone's eyes, you can see whether there is sadness or joy. In artwork, the emphasis is automatically created as soon as there are people as subjects. We instinctually are drawn towards people. Otherwise it could be a number of things that could take your attention first within the piece.

When you think of your life, you must agree that the emphasis should be on the people instead of material things. This truth is shown in art, but many people have lost this fundamental truth throughout the course of their life. They get caught up with success and materialism, and they focus on that more than the people in their lives. At the end of your life, it will be the people in it that will matter—*nothing else.* Being "rich" can't buy happiness. What brings true lasting happiness has nothing to do with material things. "Shopping Therapy" is a fleeting happiness that needs to only be repeated with more "Shopping Therapy"…

Focusing on people is never a bad idea… Another cool thing is that doing things for others and helping others is a direct flight to happiness! We immediately feel satisfaction, and with their thankfulness, we feel gratitude that we have been of service. I believe that everyone is connected by love—even when we "forget" at times.

The people around you are your greatest opportunity for learning. Relationships with other people will always be your greatest asset in life. At the beginning of the movie, *Into The Wild,* the main character explains that you don't really need other people—you really only need to have the trees and nature around you. The show is based on a true story. I tried to figure out if the movie was trying to teach me something I totally didn't believe ever in my life because I love people and being around them. I remember being a bit puzzled, thinking maybe I needed to learn to be more independent!

Well, at the end as he was dying, he wrote, "Happiness is only real when it is shared." I remember being so happy to have that verified for me once again. In art class, I have always only had two rules. *Be kind—and be kind!* In life, if you can always try your best to be kind to everyone around you, you will always be happy. Let love conquer fear… Be open to others.

A few years back, an artist I had done some framing for died in her home. No one found her until six months after she passed away. It was so sad, and her life had been at the opposite end of the spectrum of creating relationships with people. When I did the framing, she would not give me her phone number to call her when her framing was ready. She said she would phone me. She had a huge fear of letting me even have her phone number. She went so far away from love that her whole life was swallowed up by fear. She ended up starving to death because she was too scared of going out in public to get her groceries. She had shut out all her family and friends over the years. Incredibly sad…

Many people function along the spectrum between fear and love. Choose love… You will never regret choosing love. Even when you are disappointed by the behaviors of others who you love and trust, remember that it was a learning lesson. Take the lesson, forgive, forget, and move on. Their behavior arose because of their own fear and lack of understanding the "big picture," and even though it has affected you, it truly has nothing to do with you. Not everyone will disappoint you. There are wise thoughtful people with huge hearts and integrity out there to love that will love you back! Always remember to have the courage to take the risk. *Not every artwork you attempt will be perfect, but does that mean you quit creating art?* Ask yourself, *"Who suffers then?"*

"The people around you are your greatest opportunity for learning. Relationships with other people will always be your greatest asset in life."

"Love," acrylic painting, original size: 16" x 20", 2013

The emphasis is subtle in this artwork, but it is where the light hits on the left person's head and upper back. This piece portrays the loving, caring relationship between two people. It could be between children, friends, siblings, cousins, lovers, etc. It is the tolerant and nonjudgmental love of another person. You know they have your back and will always be there for you in good times and bad. They have integrity. They have always been trustworthy and been there for you.

Proportion

Proportion is the second principle of composition, and it really means that everything is in relationship to other things. There are certain "rules" to life that you can't change. Inuit people can make a coat that will fit you perfectly, based only on the size of your wrist. There are many other size rules that explain how living things have all been created in perfect proportion.

As an artist, drawing with accurate proportions takes practice and training. In your life, if you choose to make one part of your life that isn't that important bigger than everything else, it will not make sense with the rest of your life. Some proportions are not as important in artwork. For example, if you make a cloud too big or small, no one will ever notice—and it doesn't really matter. However, when drawing an eye, it has to be the right size and in proportion to the rest of the face. In your life, it works the same way. With some things, you must pay attention to the common sense rules because certain things are really important and require a larger portion of your life. For example, the people you care about need more of your time.

It takes time and maturity to figure out what people and things need more of your time and energy. These relate back to your values and morals—the lines and shapes of your initial plan. You want your choices to be in line with your heart and something that doesn't change too much. You want them to stay constant. It has to do with rules of priority and deciding what things in your life can take up the most space! The most important things need more space!

When learning art, we always work from realism. Realism teaches us the proper proportions of things. It is only after learning realism that a person can start to branch into Impressionism or abstract art to create beautiful masterpieces. Life is the same way. We often go with what we know, and we copy the happenings and lifestyles of the people around us that we have experienced in a real way.

When we do a rendition of another artist's work that we admire, we are copying his or her style. It is an excellent exercise to copy a master's work because the learning you do is huge. We have many people in our lives that we can pay attention to find out what they are doing to make their lives work so well. We have that choice. No one's life will ever be the same as anyone else's, but you will be drawn to certain people because their souls resonate with your soul. Your morals and values probably mesh.

We may not end up emulating the people close to us, but that will often be the case. If the environment you grew up in is not what you want for yourself and your children, you still have a choice about your future—and how you want to create it. Pay attention!

A boy told me that he learned the most about how to live a great life through his sister's boyfriend. He called his sister's boyfriend his best role model. We all have role models around us in our lives who have sorted out what parts of their lives need bigger proportions than others. They have figured out some "life rules" that really work! We need to pay attention and have the courage to create lives that ring true to us. We know we have that choice after seeing others around us create theirs.

How much of your life will be spent doing this or that? What will you give most of your time and effort to? Pay attention to your habits. Are they beneficial for you? Do you need to be more mindful in making choices?

> "We need to pay attention and have the courage to create lives that ring true to us. We know we have that choice after seeing others around us create theirs."

**"Renoir Tulips,"
acrylic painting,
original size: 36"
x 48", 2005**

I painted this rendition of "Tulips in a Vase" by Renoir for the Masterpiece Art Show and Sale. My art school put on this fundraiser for our field trip to Paris in 2005. For students, working from master's artwork is a huge opportunity to learn what they otherwise would miss out on. Piano players learn Beethoven's compositions for the same reason. This is why it makes sense to pay attention to what others are doing in their amazing lives! This painting reminds me of the wholesome richness of life, which we get to experience when we focus on what matters. This is when we live thoughtfully and give everything proper proportions.

Balance

Balance is the third principle of composition. When we think about it, we absolutely need to balance everything in our lives. We need morals and values, but we also need to have fun and "let loose" every once in a while. In other words, we need upright, straight lines balanced by curvy, fun ones. The same goes with shapes. You need some ugly, jutting, pointy shapes to appreciate the curved, round ones. It's important to enjoy light and faith, but in order to understand how fortunate you are, you need to experience moments of darkness too. You will realize that it is okay—and it is all for learning.

Personalities can often be described as shapes. The curving shapes are a lot friendlier, but they are probably more complicated because they tend to internalize things and have a lot more changes that are possible—and possibilities of where they are going. Straight shapes are more direct and unchanging. They are less tolerant of changes in direction and lack of direction that curving personalities seem to have. It's interesting that many relationships create balance with one another—opposites attract just as opposite colors attract and balance one other in artwork.

Artwork has to be balanced so it doesn't seem visually heavy on either side. How the artist places the lines, shapes, values, colors, texture and space is done with careful thought so that this doesn't happen.

In life, nothing is ever as dark as it seems in the moment. Black is all the colors mixed up, and there are always silver linings *(or what I like to call rainbows)* of learning hidden within each dark event. As sad as it may sound, when my brother passed away at a young age, our whole family finally understood what true love is. Kim's death gave us a greater understanding of life and an appreciation for each other. It bonded us in a way that probably would never have happened otherwise. It taught me that death is real, but the real concern for me was not death itself, but instead, not really living. My faith and ability to be at peace and content became strong when I found that place of strength within. Most religions believe that God is within you, and I learned this to be true.

I've also experienced having three different types of cancer. So I now have my black belt, yellow belt, and am working on my pink belt. I don't call them ribbons… there was a fight involved. As sad as that may sound, each time it's been a gift to really remind myself to "live". *Does that mean I focus on the dark and make sure I share my dark stories with everyone?* Absolutely not. Anyone who knows me would testify that I always tend to focus on the light. Many people would never even know I've had cancer just as I would never focus on the cold I had last week. It's just not my focus.

I do however remember asking my friend, *"WHY have I had cancer three times?"* She asked me why she had been diabetic since she was seven years old. Sometimes there aren't any answers—just the lessons you learn from the experiences. Dark times help you to understand how amazing the "light" is. They help you make a point of having it become a bigger part of your life.

In artwork, the contrast of light and dark (value) and the balancing act that happens with this creates the most powerful pieces of art. I appreciate the dark moments in life because they put things in perspective. When something big happens—like a serious health issue or a death in the family—it sheds light on the important things. They are put into priority and this focus on the light balances out the heavy darkness we may feel. We realize that all the little things we stress about on a day-to-day basis don't really matter. It allows a whole new way of seeing our lives and what truly matters. The dark moments are part of our story and what has happened to us—but we need to remember they are *NOT ACTUALLY US*! The quality and happiness of our life is not dependent on what happens to us, but rather how we respond. We decide if we will allow these stories to create shadows over our lives or if we just appreciate and pay attention to the lessons and "shedding of light" that the stories give us.

> "I appreciate the dark moments in life because they put things in perspective. When something big happens—like a serious health issue or a death in the family—it sheds light on the important things. They are put into priority and this focus on the light balances out the heavy darkness we may feel."

Light and dark have to be in balance, but so does color. Complementary colors and a variety of colors balance each other within a piece and the artist needs to make sure not to overpower the piece with too much of one color.

There also needs to be balance with texture and space—you can't have the whole piece highly detailed. Your focal point and your subject will be more detailed and the background will often be much more blurry. Your eyes can only focus on one thing at a time, and that is true in your life as well…

It is funny that cameras focus on everything unless you change the settings to macro, which is why artists who work too much from photographs will have artwork that looks flat. In your life, you can't pay attention and focus on everything. You don't have time for everything or everyone. Aristotle's quote, "A friend to all is a friend to none," explains this perfectly. Choose your friends wisely. You can't be everyone's friend—even if you're like me and love everyone.

"A Great Pair," acrylic painting, original size: 8" x 10", 2013

This artwork is symmetrical, so the visual balance is evident. "A Great Pair" speaks to what we need to create a great life, and it includes the aspirations we have for our relationships. We always need to take care of our own needs before we engage in relationships that are reciprocal in caring, thoughtfulness, and respect. We need to find partners to hold hands with for life so that we can appreciate and cherish each other's differences. These differences bring balance into our lives. We need to take the time to sort out exactly what we want in our lives. Then with the support from those around us, we will have the courage to go for it!

Movement

Movement in artwork is the illusion of movement or how our eyes move around the artwork. It is created by the way we organize the elements. It is very important that there is movement because otherwise the artwork is "stuck". We may follow bright colors first or the largest shapes, and then our eyes will move to the duller colors and smaller shapes.

In your life, there will be some things that will always be constants and big parts of your life. That doesn't mean you won't dabble in many things. This keeps your life interesting. Focus on the things in your life that you find most important. It's okay if there may be a few things that take your attention at times.

Life is like a song with choruses and verses. The chorus is the main part of your life, and the verses are the extras that keep your life whole! If you ever feel stuck in life, it can mean that you have put too much energy into one person or thing without balancing it with others. Focus on you and your health. Focus on your relationships— and then focus on your work. Be sure they are in the right order—and include all three!

You need to fill your cup first, but sometimes you can focus too much on yourself. Being too self-absorbed will never bring happiness either. The happiest people are those who shift the focus from themselves to other people. After you've taken the time to care for yourself, share the love. Move it around. *LIVE!* Never forget that love is not a noun—*it's a verb*. It takes some action!

"Focus on you and your health. Focus on your relationships—and then focus on your work. Be sure they are in the right order—and include all three!"

"Lovely Restaurant,"
acrylic painting,
original size:
36" x 48", 2012

This painting of a bustling street in Charlottetown shows a restaurant with tables on the sidewalk. There is a lot of energy, excitement, and movement. It is a place for people to come together and share their lives over beautiful suppers on moonlit evenings. The composition is perfect, and the emphasis is the light on the lamppost. Your eyes start looking at the lamppost and make their way around to look at everything. There is a lot to look at, and you will find your eyes continuing to move around this interesting piece.

Rhythm/Repetition

This is about patterns of similarity. Repetition of lines and shapes help lead your eye around the artwork. For example, your eyes will follow circular shapes around in a painting, and they will follow the same colors. Similar to music, this would be the chorus. Imagine a song that just kept changing in tempo and lyrics and never had a chorus. It would feel as though it was lacking a base structure.

In your life, traditions and events in your life repeat themselves. They give you a feeling of familiarity and contentment. This includes the friends and family that you hold close to your heart. These are people you continue to put time and effort into, and therefore sustain and maintain relationships with. They become a very treasured part of your rhythm throughout the course of your life.

In life, you have routines and things you do every day, such as brushing your teeth, praying at night, or waking up at a certain time. Having familiar things and people you can count on gives you a sense of contentment and peace. They almost give you an idea of what's going to happen next, because you become accustomed to their presence in your life.

If you notice certain patterns or ideas that keep coming up in your life, pay attention to them. Things that keep showing up can tell you a lot about your life's purpose. Life is trying to tell you something...

Oprah explained this like a thread that keeps running throughout your life. Pay attention to what it is that keeps coming up for you. It's probably one of your strengths that is so easy that you take it for granted and don't pay much attention to it. Many people miss out on their life's calling because they are not paying attention.

"A Walk In The Woods," acrylic painting, original size: 48" x 72", 2008

Nature is a beautiful place to find your own sanctuary. It is a place where you can unplug and be filled with a beautiful energy that comes from being in nature. Here is where you can slow down enough to pay attention to what things have kept coming up in your life and dream about what you want to see in your future. This painting is full of repetition. The colors and shapes continue to repeat themselves. In nature, all things repeat themselves and have a natural rhythm. That is why it's so soothing to experience this in artwork.

Variety and Unity

The sixth principal of composition—variety and unity—is the most important. There must be a feeling that nothing should be added, taken away, or changed. In artwork, this means that the parts seem to belong together, the colors harmonize, nothing is out of place, and the technique or style is harmonious with the subject and mood. This is close to the final stage.

There are some tricks to help you (looking at it from a distance, putting it away for a few days, etc.). That way, you will have fresh eyes to see if anything is missing or doesn't feel quite right. In life, you can sometimes feel that something needs to change, but you can be so close to yourself that it is impossible to see the things you need to change. Others can see it easily, but it can be hard for you. This is why we need to share our lives with others and be close enough to trust them to shed some light on our lives and the things we need work on or change.

If we are able to develop relationships where we have total trust and openness, we will be able to appreciate when others can help us out because they can see our lives from a completely fresh perspective. These friends and family are golden. Even when they tell us what we might not want to hear at first, we need to be thankful for their words. Those words are not always easy to say…

> "If we are able to develop relationships where we have total trust and openness, we will be able to appreciate when others can help us out because they can see our lives from a completely fresh perspective."

In my art classes, I never work on the student's artwork. When they are finished, it is 100 percent theirs. I give direction, but I never touch their paintbrushes or pencils to paint or draw. The only thing I do sometimes is help them to see by finding "points" when they are having difficulties finding the initial lines and shapes.

In life it is similar— you can't actually solve anyone else's problems. You can give them direction, but ultimately we all are responsible for ourselves. Only we can make changes in our lives so things are unified, and yet have enough variety to keep us fulfilled and excited about life. The beautiful part is that we have the power to create exactly the life we envision!

"Artistic Beauty,"
acrylic painting,
original size: 16"
x 20", 2003

This painting makes me think of Michelangelo. It takes me back to a time when people put a lot of effort into making things beautiful and people appreciated great artwork— energy and resources were freely spent on creating beauty. When you are in a beautiful environment, you receive energy and feel a lot better about your life in general. Variety in artwork can be huge, but the unifying element is that it all adds up to a positive feeling. Original art adds warmth and a feeling of *welcome* into your space. I have been so blessed to have so many people tell me how much my artwork in their home enriches their day-to-day lives.

Summary

If you can put any of this understanding into either your art or your life, it will change the way you approach your life. There is so much to learn, and it is so exciting. If you've never taken an art class, it's time you enrolled in one. While you're there, learning about life is also bound to happen!

When I am teaching art, I constantly say, *"Look, look, look and draw a little."* In life, this means, *"Learn, learn, learn—and act on it a little."* Just five minutes of sketching a day can improve your drawing skills dramatically. Just five minutes a day of passionately practicing or envisioning your future life or traits you would like to enhance in yourself will make a huge difference.

You can get your images for art from looking at objects in the real world, looking at pictures of subjects, or using your imagination or memory *(I call this "film")*. The best way to learn when you are beginning as an art student is by using real-world objects. This is true with life too. You can learn and follow what has worked for other people, but until you listen to your heart and do what YOU need to do, you will never have complete satisfaction in life. Take every teachable moment as it comes—*and be in the moment*. As soon as you quit learning, you become stagnate. Your life and artwork become boring. Keep learning—stay open to seeing life in a different way so you can continue to grow and create the life you want. Use your imagination and your memory of what created happy feelings to keep a fresh perspective and a sense of adventure…

> **"Just five minutes a day of passionately practicing or envisioning your future life or a trait you would like to enhance in yourself will make a huge difference."**

At the end of a new medium art workshop, I give certificates to the students. I always say it's like a "license" for their medium, and the most important thing is that they don't speed while doing their art. The same is true in life. We really need to slow down and enjoy the journey. Anytime we are rushing, we are not able to enjoy as we go. To this day, I have kept a beautiful broken watch that I wear every now and then to remind myself of this. It was serendipitous that the glass face broke first and then the hands broke off at a time when I most needed to learn this. When someone asks me what time it is, I show my watch and say,

"The time is now. So ENJOY it!" It adds some fun and is a bit of a running joke with some of my friends when I wear that watch!

> **"We really need to slow down and enjoy the journey. Anytime we are rushing, we are not able to enjoy as we go."**

What about mistakes? An artist friend of mine, Frank Sudol, told me that mistakes are for learning. If you are not making mistakes, you are not learning. Welcome mistakes because that is where you do the bulk of your real learning. When you are floundering, you are most likely doing your best growth and development—even though it is hard sometimes. Think of when a child is learning to walk and how much they fall over. They start to learn about balance and what they will do the next time so they don't hurt themselves again. They don't quit trying. They just learn and move on.

When drawing, mistakes are likely, but I always teach my students to keep drawing until they get what they want *and then* to erase what they don't want! I teach them to focus on what's right and keep building on that. I tell them not to worry about the mistakes—other than to use them as guides for what they don't want!

Another important reminder is to *never forget to focus on the positive…* If you focus on the positive in art, it seems like the negative takes care of itself. It becomes the background that doesn't matter in the end. You are always in control of how your life looks, and focusing on the positive makes that part more important and influential. This is where gratitude comes in. Everything has to move in a positive direction when you approach your art and your life with a grateful spirit. Pay attention to what's right! You may have heard that energy flows where attention goes. This is true… You want to keep your attention on the things that are positive that matter!

> **"This is where gratitude comes in. Everything has to move in a positive direction when you approach your art and your life with a grateful spirit. Pay attention to what's right!"**

When teaching art, I often compare it to learning piano. At first, we use images of art that have been done before for reference (like a Monet for example). When "learning the notes", you work on techniques and style.

Often, the first images you will gravitate toward will tell you the truth about your own style. Of course, it won't be exact, but it will give you a good indication of which style you already have within yourself. Over time, you will learn to create your own originals—through advanced instruction. This can be by setting up your own still life or learning to take your own photographs and putting your own style into these images. I compare it to learning a Beethoven piece and then some day sitting down to compose your own piece.

The learning part before composing is crucial. You need to learn theory and gain a better understanding of the elements and principles of art, which will enable you to create your own originals. You can go ahead and copy the work of others forever, but it doesn't help you develop your own style and understanding as an artist. It keeps you an "art student" rather than an "artist" who can create your own original work. Because of copyright laws, if you ever want to sell your artwork, it's important to learn how to create your own originals.

In your own personal life, the same is true. When you are younger, you often find yourself copying the actions and ideas of others. These are your role models, and it is beneficial to have them in your life. As you get older, you realize that you can learn your *own* truths and live your own life. This is exciting! All you need is a little bravery and confidence to get you going. *BELIEVE* in your dreams and *GET DREAMING!* Expect only the best. Believe in yourself. *BE yourself—you truly are an original!*

Salvador Dali said, "Everything is either easy or impossible." People often don't believe this, but if you think about it, anything that you learn and master will become easy sooner or later. *What do you think? What do you choose to believe?*

"Harvest Time," acrylic painting, original size: 24" x 36", 2006

"Harvest Time" signifies a harvest of efforts put into one's life. The investment of time and effort is worth all the payoffs in the future. Sometimes it just feels like a lot of hard work. Van Gogh said, "To get to the essence of things, one has to work long and hard." This is similar to what my husband always says, "You get what you put in!" Go for it. Dream and take steps toward your goals. You will be pleased you put in the effort!

Finishing Touches

Near the end of an art piece, an artist needs to spend time on a few little finishing touches. It's where the smallest things can make a big difference in the overall look of a piece, but it is almost impossible to do alone because you are so connected to your work.

Paul Gardener said, "A painting is never finished. It simply stops in interesting places." *Will artwork ever be totally perfect?* No. Perfection is not possible. There's always something to continue to work on, and the same is true in life. During finishing touches, you need another person who is experienced and educated to help you. In art class, students have me take a peek and give them advice on the last touches, such as a last magical brush stroke or added color. In life, that may mean relying on a friend or someone in your family to help you. Someone you trust will give you good advice. Some people prefer to hire a life coach, and that's awesome. Do whatever works for you!

I've had the most amazing things happen in my life. In high school, our choir made an album and I have a solo recorded on it. My husband and I flew a private jet to our honeymoon in Los Angeles, built a cabin for family time when our children were little, took our children out of school for a year and went on a world trip, and have recently built a house with an art studio of my dreams. I also quit a secure teaching job to adventure into the career of my heart without looking back. Three different people gave me a DVD of *The Secret* when it first came out because they said it reminded them of me. I am fortunate to have been brought up with the mindset of being positive and expecting favorable things to happen, but I also believe that anyone can learn how. You can start a new canvas anytime to create exactly what you want! I'm so excited for you!

Here's a little finishing touch I don't want you to miss out on. *Have you ever made a mistake or had a negative incident happen that you had no control over, and you've replayed it in your mind, continuing to have regrets and sadness long after the fact?* You need to quit playing old sad tracks and start playing the tracks of your future—bright, bold, and full of your wildest dreams! The past is over. If you've done what you can to make things right—and you've learned from it—that's all you can ask for. It's time to start living in the now *(the present that it is)* and create more of what you want for the future by dreaming and envisioning! That is where your absolute best life is!

How great is right now and what are you looking forward to? Think about your future and be excited for it, but don't forget to give yourself opportunities in the present to take in life through your senses in the best way possible to enjoy each and every moment! These moments count and you have the power to create your own happiness whenever you want! Enjoy… *Some questions to ask yourself— the list is endless: Do you pay attention to the mood and lyrics in songs? Do you think about what foods you put in your mouth? Have you tried treating yourself to essential oils in your bath? Do you spend some time creating a beautiful environment in your home so it's uplifting? Do you take time to create your very own sanctuary in your mind and in your home?…*

When teaching art, I often refer to us teachers as being the lifeguards. As you journey into the world of learning to draw and paint, we compare it to setting out to sea. Along the way, you definitely know you will hit some big waves. Sometimes this is when you need to have your teacher (lifeguard) to help you out. Nothing is too hard, and nothing is impossible without help. This brings me back to my faith—I can't imagine life without faith. It is like a lifejacket for when things get rough, which they surely will.

I have been lucky to have my faith verified to me a number of times. The first few times were when I was having trouble in my personal life. As always, along with my many thanks, I was praying before bed for answers. Three times, really important prayers have been answered at three o'clock in the morning. I wake up with the exact words I need to hear. Every time, it has felt like a true enlightenment and has been a total transformation and change of perspective.

I think it is rare to have your faith verified in a concrete way. I was lucky enough to have this happen to me once. This next story was a very special moment in my life that I need to share. We all have our own personal spiritual journeys, and this just happened to be part of mine.

Our family was staying in a cabin in Australia during our yearlong trip. One evening, we were watching coverage of the pope passing away on television. It made me quite sad, and I wondered why I could be so sad. I started to wonder: *Why am I Lutheran and not Catholic? Why haven't our kids gone to Catholic school? Why are there so many religions that only seem to separate people?*

As I went to sleep, I said a little prayer. At the usual answer time (three o'clock in the morning), I awoke to a voice. "It doesn't matter which religion you are—what matters is the intensity of your relationship with Jesus Christ." Some quieter words went on to say something about my chosen faith not really mattering because we are all going to the same place. That was so exciting for me. The words filled me with contentment because I always kind of had that idea but always wondered because it seemed like being Catholic would have been easier for some reason… I went to sleep shortly after.

In the morning I had an experience that I will never ever forget. I was in the bathroom buckling my belt. All of a sudden, I heard a loud "ting" as if something metal hit the floor. I assumed it was my belt buckle at first. I knew I heard it land near the garbage can so I check the floor close to there. My Saint Christopher that my mom gave me before our trip, was on the floor. I immediately went to grab the chain around my neck, thinking it must have been broken. When I felt my necklace, I realized that my cross was still on, and the chain was totally intact. So then I checked out the loop on the Saint Christopher, and it too was intact. There was no way that I knew how it could have ever come off… and with such force! I was in a bit of shock and completely disheveled.

Immediately, my whole body started to shake. I quickly and instinctually sat on the toilet *(it was either that or the floor!)* and brought my hands together in prayer. I was totally moved, but also a little freaked out at the same time... I told my husband right away, and he explained it in the nicest way. I love his perspective on this. He said I should be thankful to have an experience like that because most people never do. We had talked about my dream that morning, and his explanation was that God was just telling me that as a Christian, as long as I have Jesus as central in my life, I don't really need Saint Christopher to protect me. It was almost like someone was saying, *"This is so you don't forget what I told you in the middle of the night."*

To this day, I still find it hard to believe that happened to me, but I will always be thankful.

Faith is totally unique for each and every person. This is just like when people are drawing a still life around a table and looking at the same thing, everyone's artwork will look totally different. No two people's artwork will ever be alike—and neither will their faith. How we approach it is different, and our perspective is totally different. We all see things differently, learn things differently, and experience our lives differently… That is what makes our lives so exciting and unique!

The coolest thing I've witnessed that even comes close to my thoughts about us all going to the same place was in Bali, Indonesia. All the different faiths had built their buildings in a circle and shared a parking lot in the center. There were temples, mosques, churches, etc. My heart felt warm seeing it—like everything was right in the world. I long for the day when we quit separating people and creating judgment and hostility based on faith, skin color, sexuality, cultural heritage, etc. We all need to know that we will always be more alike than we will ever be different.

Enjoy! Life is a masterpiece to create. Live it as only you can! You are an original, and there will never be *anyone* exactly like you! Listen to you heart. Only you can make it great! Have faith—and go for it! You were born for a reason. Figure it out, live it, and envision the best. You deserve to live a life that is absolutely amazing! Your life will become what you think it should be so go "BIG." You truly have the choice, and even though it may seem like a big ocean out there, the world is your oyster...

"Enjoy! Life is a masterpiece to create. Live it as only you can!"

"Courage at Gethsemane,"
acrylic painting,
original size:
36" x 48", 2012

The most heart-wrenching thing about this moment in time was when Jesus was hanging on the cross and he looked up to God and said, "Forgive them, Father, for they know not what they do." Forgiveness of others is huge, but forgiving yourself is important too. Have the courage to acknowledge your mistakes, learn from them, and then love and accept yourself in order to have the freedom to create and live the life of your dreams.

About the Author

Christina Thoen is an author, artist, and teacher who immerses herself in art, instilling the love of art to students in her private art school and creating masterpieces in her studio. She has been creating and selling her artwork for more than thirty years. She lives with her husband Lorne in Prince Albert, Saskatchewan, Canada. They have three boys Anthony, Nathan, and Quinten.

After quitting teaching in the school system in 1995, Christina started her business—Christina's Framing, Gallery, and Art School—where she sells her artwork and teaches art classes to more than 150 students per week. Students drive from all over, including La Ronge, Saskatoon, and Nipawin for weekly classes. One student commuted more than three hundred kilometers from Stanley Mission for years.

Christina has been commissioned by corporations and private collectors worldwide and has sold hundreds of paintings over the years, carrying little inventory at any given time. Her personal gallery where she sells her artwork was voted as one of the best places to buy art in Saskatchewan in the *Prairies North* magazine in November 2013. This year, she was voted "Best of the Best" for best local Artist in the city of Prince Albert and area.

Christina wrote this book to share her knowledge and help people learn about creating a great life. In one of those *everything-happens-for-a reason* coincidental moments, her camper van broke down outside of Saskatoon. Because of this, a week later, she ended up in Chicago with one of her soul sisters to attend a conference.

In Chicago, she became an Infinite Possibilities Certified Trainer. The program is inspired by Mike Dooley's *Infinite Possibilities: The Art of Living Your Dreams*. She is super excited to offer workshops in helping people move forward with creating their dream lives through this amazing program, which also fits perfectly with her book.

Please visit her website below if you want to see more of her artwork and/or to learn more about registering for retreat workshops at Christina's Life School and/or classes and workshops at Christina's Art School.

www.christinathoen.com

"Ocean View," acrylic painting, original size: 48" x 60", 2013

This painting from Prince Edward Island shows so much depth. It is as if you are standing in a beautiful field of flowers and looking out toward the ocean. Try to envision yourself there right now. Feel the air, smell the flowers, and take it all in. The world is your oyster. *You* choose. Make it your best. You deserve it! Much love to you…